VALLEYS
Psalm 23

Dr. Larry Petton

2017

Elm Springs, Arkansas

*The cover photo taken by Larry Petton
Durango, Colorado*

About the Author

Dr. Larry Petton has been the Senior Pastor of Cross Pointe Community Church in Tontitown, Arkansas since 2005. Larry has served as Senior Pastor of 6 churches in Texas and Arkansas and also as a Professor in two Christian colleges. In addition, he has been a Corporate Chaplain since 2005. Dr. Petton is the author of five books which are available on Amazon.

The Cancer of Unforgiveness

Daddy, What Does It Feel Like to Die?

God, Why Is This Happening To America?

When Lucifer Left Heaven

Valleys

BLESSING on this BOOK

Father, I give you this book. It is yours. Do whatever You choose to do with this writing. Be glorified in its content and may it be totally in line with Your Word. Use this book to encourage those who are walking through a dark, lonely valley. In Jesus' Name. Amen.

DEDICATION

To Katie and Andy, God has given me the pleasure of being your father and serving as a shepherd in your life. I am so proud of you. I love you both with all of my heart and thank God for you.

QUOTES on TRIALS

"Trials should not surprise us, or cause us to doubt God's faithfulness. Rather, we should actually be glad for them. God sends trials to strengthen our trust in Him so that our faith will not fail. Our trials keep us trusting; they burn away our self-confidence and drive us to our Savior."

- Edmund Clowney

"There are two ways of getting out of a trial. One is simply to try to get rid of the trial, and be thankful when it is over. The other is to recognize the trial as a challenge from God to claim a larger blessing than we have ever had, and to hail it with delight as an opportunity of obtaining a larger measure of divine grace."

- A. B. Simpson

"You may readily judge whether you are a child of God or a hypocrite by seeing in what direction your soul turns in seasons of severe trial. The hypocrite flies to the world and finds a sort of comfort there. But the child of God runs to his Father and expects consolation only from the Lord's hand."

- Charles Spurgeon

"To learn strong faith is to endure great trials. I have learned my faith by standing firm amid severe testings."

- George Mueller

"Trouble is one of God's great servants because it reminds us how much we continually need the Lord."

- Jim Cymbala

"Trials come to prove and to improve us."

- Augustine

"I never had a trial I wanted to have, but I never had trial I wasn't glad I had."

- Jack Hyles

"The man who has an easy way through life, will be spiritually weak, flabby and impoverished. He won't be able to do all that God wants him to do. But the one who has gone through trials and testing successfully, will be strong and capable of doing all the will of God."

- Zac Poonen

"It is of no use to say to men, "Let not your heart be troubled," unless you finish the verse and say, "Believe in God, believe also in Christ.""

- Alexander MacLaren

"If we desire our faith to be strengthened, we should not shrink from opportunities where our faith may be tried, and, therefore, through trial, be strengthened."

- George Mueller

"Anger and bitterness are two noticeable signs of being focused on self and not trusting God's sovereignty in your life. When you believe that God causes all things to work together for good to those who belong to Him and love Him, you can respond to trials with joy instead of anger or bitterness."

- John C. Broger

"Faith is like insurance. It needs to be wholly in place before there's a crisis."

- Pamela Christian

"As I look back over fifty years of ministry, I recall innumerable tests, trials and times of crushing pain. But, through it all, the Lord has proven faithful, loving, and totally true to all his promises."

- David Wilkerson

"So surely as the stars are fashioned by His hands, and their orbits fixed by Him, so surely are our trials allotted to us: He has ordained their season and their place, their intensity and the effect they shall have upon us."

- Charles Spurgeon

"We are so easily entangled in earthly affairs and so easily consumed with the desire for those things that do not last. We will not live on this earth forever, so even our trials should be viewed in the light of eternity."

- Theodore Epp

"You will have no test of faith that will not fit you to be a blessing if you are obedient to the Lord. I never had a trial but when I got out of the deep river I found some poor pilgrim on the bank that I was able to help by that very experience."

— A. B. Simpson

"Never let go of what you DO KNOW because of something you DON'T KNOW!"

— Unknown

"In the secret of God's tabernacle no enemy can find us, and no troubles can reach us. The pride of man and the strife of tongues find no entrance into the pavilion of God. The secret of His presence is a more secure refuge than a thousand Gibraltars. I do not mean that no trials come. They may come in abundance, but they cannot penetrate into the sanctuary of the soul and we may dwell in perfect peace even in the midst of life's fiercest storms."

— Hannah Whitall Smith

"We are always on the anvil; by trials God is shaping us for higher things."

- Henry Ward Beecher

"No physician ever weighed out medicine to his patients with half so much care and exactness as God weighs out to us every trial. Not one grain too much does He ever permit to be put in the scale."

- Henry Ward Beecher

"Never stumble over what's behind you."

- Jack Wellman

BIBLE VERSES on TRIALS

"Trust in the LORD with all your heart, and lean not on your own understanding; in all your ways acknowledge Him, and He shall direct your paths."
Proverbs 3:5-6 (NKJV)

"For I reckon that the sufferings of this present time are not worthy to be compared with the glory which shall be revealed in us." Romans 8:18 (KJV)

"Blessed are they which are persecuted for righteousness' sake: for theirs is the kingdom of heaven. Blessed are ye, when men shall revile you, and persecute you, and shall say all manner of evil against you falsely, for my sake. Rejoice, and be exceeding glad: for great is your reward in heaven: for so persecuted they the prophets which were before you." Matthew 5:10-12 (KJV)

"The LORD is good, a refuge in times of trouble.
He cares for those who trust in him." Nahum 1:7 (NIV)

"That the trial of your faith, being much more precious than of gold that perishes, though it be tried with fire, might be found unto praise and honor and glory at the appearing of Jesus Christ:" 1 Peter 1:7 (KJV)

"Beloved, think it not strange concerning the fiery trial which is to try you, as though some strange thing happened unto you: but rejoice, inasmuch as ye are partakers of Christ's sufferings; that, when His glory shall be revealed, ye may be glad also with exceeding joy."
1 Peter 4:12-13 (KJV)

"These things I have spoken unto you, that in me ye might have peace. In the world ye shall have tribulation: but be of good cheer; I have overcome the world"   John 16:33 (KJV)

"And they overcame him by the blood of the Lamb, and by the word of their testimony; and they loved not their lives unto the death."   Revelation 12:11 (KJV)

"Who shall separate us from the love of Christ? Shall tribulation, or distress, or persecution, or famine, or nakedness, or peril, or sword? As it is written, for thy sake we are killed all the day long; we are accounted as sheep for the slaughter. Nay, in all these things we are more than conquerors through Him that loved us."
Romans 8:35-37 (KJV)

"For we have not an high priest which cannot be touched with the feeling of our infirmities; but was in all points tempted like as we are, yet without sin."
Hebrews 4:15 (KJV)

"For our light affliction, which is but for a moment, works for us a far more exceeding and eternal weight of glory;"
1 Corinthians 4:17 (KJV)

*Special thanks to my beautiful
editor & wife, Rosanne.
Love you.*

VALLEYS

Psalm 23

PSALM 23

New King James Version (NKJV)
A Psalm of David.

23 The Lord is my shepherd;
I shall not want.

2
He makes me to lie down in green pastures;
He leads me beside the still waters.

3
He restores my soul;
He leads me in the paths of righteousness
For His name's sake.

4
Yea, though I walk through the valley of the
shadow of death,
I will fear no evil;
For You are with me;
Your rod and Your staff, they comfort me.

5
You prepare a table before me in the presence of my enemies;
You anoint my head with oil;
My cup runs over.

6
Surely goodness and mercy shall follow me
All the days of my life;
And I will dwell in the house of the Lord
Forever.

Psalm 23 is the most popular chapter of the Bible. It has been shared at funerals, deathbeds, hospitals and in places of worship for over 2000 years. It is one of the most beautiful pieces of literature known to man.

Harriet Ward Beecher once said, "Psalm 23 has charmed more griefs to rest than all the philosophy of the world. It has remanded to their dungeon more felon thoughts, more black doubts, more thieving sorrows, than there are sands on the seashore. It has sung courage to the army of the disappointed. It has poured balm and consolation into the heart of the sick."

Charles Spurgeon, the great preacher and theologian from England, said about this great chapter that **"Psalm 23 is the Nightingale of the Psalms."** The nightingale is a rare bird that sings its love songs during the darkest night just as this wonderful writing whispers hope into our hearts in the midst of the valleys of life.

Psalm 23 is divided into three parts:

First, David takes us into the Glen.
Then he takes us down into the Gorge.
And, finally, on to the Glory.

*In the first part of the psalm, David introduces us to One who can take care of our **Frailty**; then to the One who can take care of our **Foes**; and finally to the One who can take care of our **Future**.*

But, of all the ways we can divide this psalm, this is the best: "The secret of a happy life, a happy death, a happy eternity."

It's interesting to note that each of the Old Testament names for Jehovah is seen in Psalm 23:

Jehovah-Jireh – "The Lord will provide" (Gen. 22:13-14).

Jehovah-Rapha – "The Lord will heal or restore" (Ex. 15:26).

Jehovah-Shalom – "The Lord our peace" (Judges 6:24)

Jehovah-Tsidkenu – "The Lord our righteousness" (Jer. 23:6)

Jehovah-Shammah – "The Lord is there" (Ezek. 48:35)

Jehovah-Nissi – "The Lord our banner" (Ex. 17:8-15)

Jehovah-Rohi – "The Lord my shepherd" (Ps. 23:1).

It is a familiar idea throughout the Bible that the Lord is a Shepherd to His people. The idea begins as early as the Book of Genesis, where Moses called the Lord "the Shepherd, the Stone of Israel" (Genesis 49:24).

In Psalms 28:9, David invited the Lord to shepherd the people of Israel to "bear them up forever".

Isaiah 40:11 tells us that the Lord will "feed His flock like a shepherd; He will gather the lambs with His arm."

The Lord is a Shepherd. But can you say that He is your Shepherd?

THE SHEPHERD TRILOGY

It is significant that Psalm 23 is situated where it is in Scripture. Psalms 22-24 are known as the Shepherd Trilogy because these three chapters point to the three-fold Shepherd ministry of Jesus Christ to His followers.

Psalm 22 – Jesus is the GOOD SHEPHERD who died for the sheep. *This chapter is a portrait of the Cross and begins with the famous quote of the Savior as He died for our sins on Calvary: "My God, my God, why have You forsaken Me?" It is a foreshadowing of the Savior who died for His sheep as He said of Himself in John 10:11: "I am the Good Shepherd. The Good Shepherd lays down his life for the sheep."*

Ps. 23 – Jesus is the GREAT SHEPHERD who lives for the sheep. *All of the verbs in Psalm 23 are in the present tense, describing the One who lives for His sheep and takes care of their every need. He can lead us through the "valley of the shadow of death" because He has conquered death by His resurrection from the grave to prove that He is God in the flesh! The writer of Hebrews spoke of Jesus the Great Shepherd as a fulfilment of this prophetic chapter:*

Hebrews 13:20: "Now may the God of peace, who, through the blood of the eternal covenant, brought back from the dead our Lord Jesus, that great Shepherd of the sheep."

Ps. 24 – Jesus is the CHIEF SHEPHERD who returns for the sheep. *Psalm 24 ends with a question: "Who is this King of Glory?" Then, David supplies the answer that echoes in the heart of every true believer in Christ:* **"Let Him come in!"** *Clearly, this is a portrait of the coming Messiah, Jesus Christ, who will one day come to the earth and reign as King.*

The first time He came to suffer and die for our sins. The second time He is coming to reign as Sovereign King. The Lamb will one day be the Lion!

Simon Peter points to that great day when Jesus shall return to set up His Kingdom on the Earth in I Peter 5:4: "And when the Chief Shepherd appears, you will receive the crown of glory that will never fade away."

**Jesus is the Good Shepherd who DIED for the sheep.
Jesus is the Great Shepherd who LIVES for the sheep.
Jesus is the Chief Shepherd who COMES for the sheep.**

My mother used to sing this great old song with such amazing harmony. We sang this quartet-style song together at home around the piano. We sang it again at Mom's funeral as we rejoiced at her total healing in the Presence of God.

WHAT A DAY THAT WILL BE

*What a day that will be,
When my Jesus I shall see.
And I look upon His face
The One who saved me by His grace!*

*When He takes me by the hand
And leads me through the Promised Land
What a day, glorious day that will be.*

WHAT DO THE SHEEP HAVE?

*Charles Spurgeon said that before a man can truly say, "The Lord is my shepherd", he must first feel himself to be a sheep by nature, "for he cannot know that God is his Shepherd unless he feels in himself that he **has the nature of a sheep**." He must relate to a sheep in its foolishness and its dependency on the Shepherd.*

The Sheep of Psalm 23 are loved, cared for, protected and well-fed. Notice the things the Shepherd gives the sheep:

Rest (v. 2)

Life (v. 3)

Guidance (v. 2, 3)

Security (v. 4-6)

The Shepherd knows each sheep by name, and they know His voice. He speaks to His sheep. Do you hear His voice in your heart?

"My sheep hear My voice, and I know them, and they follow Me; and I give eternal life to them, and they will never perish; and no one will snatch them out of My hand" (John 10: 27-28).

What is the first thing He speaks to our hearts?
Psalm 23:1 – "The Lord is my Shepherd, I shall not want." What does that mean?

"I shall not want" means, "All my needs are supplied by the Lord, my Shepherd." Not my greed, but my need.

"I shall not want" means, "I decide to not desire more than what the Lord, my Shepherd, has to give me".

You might say that the phrase, "I shall not want" is the theme for the entire chapter of Psalm 23:

In v. 2: "I shall not want" for rest and refreshment.

In v. 3: "I shall not want" for restoration & righteousness.

In v. 4: "I shall not want" for protection in times of trouble.

In v. 5: "I shall not want" for provision even in the wilderness.

In v. 6: "I shall not want" for a home to go to at the end of the day.

MY VISIT TO A SHEEP FARM

As I prepared for this book, I had the privilege of visiting the sheep farm of Steve Brannan in Wesley, Arkansas. What a great lesson in understanding the Sheep and the Shepherd from Psalm 23 this was to my soul. Here are some pictures of this special experience.

Holding a newborn lamb

The Sheep Dog guarding the flock

The Goat in the midst of the Sheep

*The Shepherd, Steve Brannan, nursing
a sick little lamb*

CAST DOWN SHEEP

David cried out in Psalm 43:5 and said,

**Why are you cast down, O my soul?
And why are you disquieted within me?
Hope in God;
For I shall yet praise Him,
The help of my countenance and my God."**

David was depressed and discouraged as he ran for his life from jealous King Saul. However, the term he uses ("cast down") comes from the language of a shepherd. As you know, David served as a shepherd for years as a young man before God called him to be King of Israel.

David knew that when a sheep is cast down, it is flat on its back, unable to get up. Have you ever been in a situation like that? Have you ever been on your back looking up to God and wondering where He was?

*When a shepherd came along and found a sheep that was **cast down**, he knew that it was for one of 3 reasons:*

1. ***Overweight*** *– the sheep might be overweight by eating too much or eating the wrong food. Sometimes we feed ourselves on the wrong spiritual diet and it brings depression to our souls.*

2. ***Looking for Soft Places*** *– sometimes sheep will find a nice, soft, hollow spot and lie down. The rest is great, but the soft spot becomes a trap and the sheep is unable to get on its feet. Don't look for a cushy spot in life to serve the Lord. He calls us to a Cross to follow Him.*

3. ***Wool madded with mud*** *– a sheep can actually get stuck in the mud when the dirt sticks in the thick wool. In the Bible, wool is a symbol of our selfish, sinful nature. In fact, the High Priest could not wear wool in the Tabernacle in the Presence of the Lord.*

*When a child of God allows their **"wool to get dirty"** and sin becomes stockpiled in the heart without confession and repentance, he may fall into pit that he created himself. Many have the idea that, when that happens, God is angry at His child and abandons them.*

But that is not our Shepherd. Jesus described the Father in Luke 15 as the one who seeks the lost lamb, pursues the lost coin and never gives up on the lost, prodigal son.

THE VALLEY OF THE SHADOW OF DEATH

Psalm 23:4 is one of the most unique verses in the Bible. It is about walking through valleys. Valleys are low places in life where we learn to grow. I am convinced that God is the Creator of valleys, though it took me a while to get that message! Let's take a word by word analytical look at this great verse:

"THOUGH"

I have never thought about how important the word, "though", is in Scripture. It is a word that means, "in spite of the fact". Here are some key verses in Scripture using the word, "though".

Job said, "THOUGH he slay me, yet I will serve Him" (Job 13:15).

David said, "God is our refuge and strength, an ever-present help in trouble. Therefore, we will not fear, THOUGH the mountains be removed, and the mountains fall into the sea" (Psalm 46:1-2).

God said to Isaiah, "THOUGH your sins be as scarlet, they shall be as white as snow" (Isaiah 1:18).

"WALK"

David said, "Yea, though I WALK through the valley."

The Christian life is a walk with the Lord through the valleys and to the mountain top. Psalm 23 describes the journey of sheep which walk with their Shepherd through the valley to the green pastures on the top of the plateau prepared for them.

There are so many great verses in Scripture which talk about our walk:

Isaiah 40:31

But they that wait upon the LORD shall renew their strength; they shall mount up with wings as eagles; they shall run, and not be weary; and they shall walk, and not faint.

Amos 3:3
Can two walk together, except they be agreed?

2 Corinthians 5:7
For we walk by faith, not by sight.

Ephesians **5:2**
And walk in love, as Christ also hath loved us, and hath given Himself for us an offering and a sacrifice to God for a sweet-smelling savour.

Colossians **2:6**
As ye have therefore received Christ Jesus the Lord, so walk ye in Him:

1 John 1:7
But if we walk in the light, as He is in the light, we have fellowship one with another, and the blood of Jesus Christ His Son cleanseth us from all sin.

WALKING *implies several things:*

- *You have to have life.*
- *You are moving either forward or backward.*
- *You have to take one step at a time.*
- *You need the light to see your path.*
- *You do best when you walk with an experienced Guide.*

All of these things point to our life in Christ. We are walking with Him, following Him and needing to stay in the light to see the path.

When we think of the "PATH" He has prepared for our lives, it makes so much sense when we see something unique about the phrase, "He leads me in the paths of righteousness for His name's sake" (Psalm 23:3).

THINK ABOUT THIS.
A possible translation of the Hebrew word for "paths" could be the phrase, "Orbits of righteousness." Very interesting. Just as the Earth orbits around the Sun in the path ordained for it by the Lord Himself, so, we orbit around Jesus, the Sun of Righteousness (Malachi 4:2), in the path the Father has specifically laid out for our lives.

But, wait, can you imagine what would happen if the planets went off their God-ordained path? There would be chaos in the universe!!!

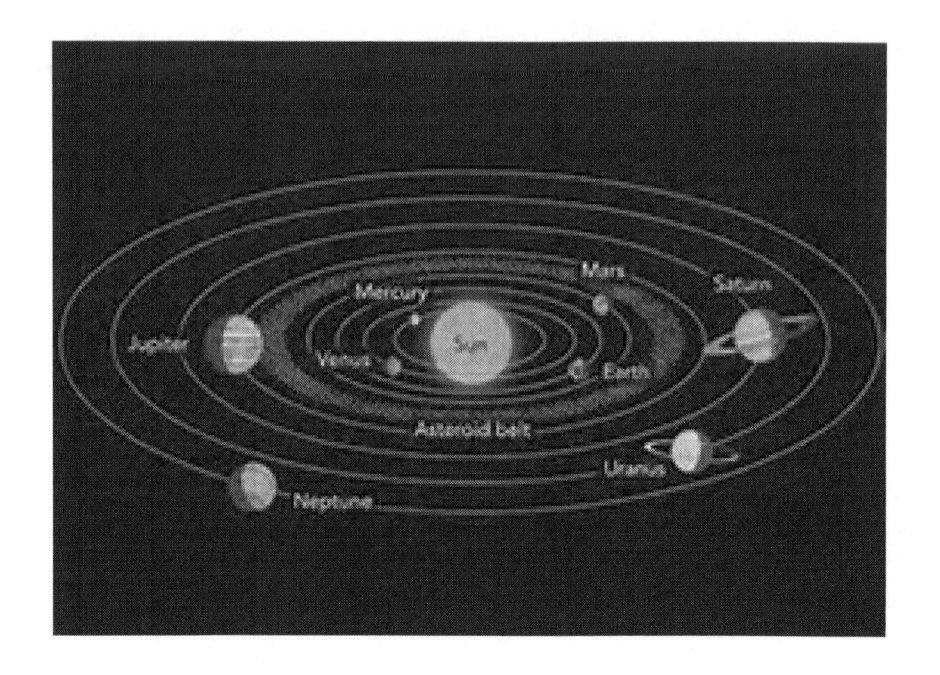

What happens to us when we get off the path that God has set for us in His Word? The end result is chaos, just like in the lives of Samson, Saul and Simon Peter in Scripture. Many more names of biblical heroes could be mentioned from Scripture. I am so glad that the Bible paints the heroes of faith "warts and all". The Bible does not glorify man, but God. This is another confirmation that it is not the word of man, but the very Word of God.

"THE VALLEY"

Valleys are low places between mountain tops. It is amazing how much God says in Scripture about valleys and how many key events in the life of His leaders in the Old Testament happened in valleys.

Here are few examples of valleys found in the Bible for you to think about:

1. The Valley of Siddim

The valley of Siddim is the very spot where the cities of Sodom and Gomorrah were. We know what happened there. God looked down and saw the wickedness of those cities and said, "I am going to rain fire and brimstone on them" (Genesis 19). This is a valley where sin abounded. This represents a valley in our lives, the valley of SIN.

2. The Valley of Eschol

Eschol is located just inside the Promised Land. Do you recall the grapes of Eschol? The Israelites came to the door of the Promised Land at Kadesh-Barnea and they appointed twelve spies (Numbers 13).

Those twelve spies went over into the Promised Land. They said it was a land that flowed with milk and honey. They brought back some grapes that were so big that it took two men to carry one bunch. But, tragically, they made a wrong choice in the **VALLEY of DECISION!**

They chose to die in defeat in the desert instead of marching to victory in the Promised Land!

3. The Valley of Elah

Elah is where David looked out and heard Goliath shout his challenges across the valley. David took his slingshot and faced Goliath in the valley of Elah. There he slew Goliath. It is the VALLEY of BATTLES. Are you in the heat of battle? You are living in the Valley of Elah.

4. The Valley of Achor

Achor is the VALLEY of CHASTENING. Achor is the valley where Achan was stoned to death for lying to God and stealing from God. The Lord said, "Do not take anything that is in Jericho."

He paid a dear price for selfishness and greed.

Are you hiding something from God? Are you living in the Valley of Achor?

5. The Valley of Gehenna

Gehenna was the garbage dump of Jerusalem. It was a place of death. Many scholars believe it is the Valley of the shadow of DEATH mentioned in Psalm 23. Have you lost a loved one? Are you nearing the gates of death in your own life? You may be near to the Valley of Gehenna.

6. The Valley of Jezreel

The Valley of Jezreel is important in the Bible because in that valley a war shall be fought at the end of the age (Ezekiel 38-39, Revelation 20). There the armies of the world will be gathered together in the great end-time battle called Armageddon. We are nearing closer and closer to that Valley each day.

AN OVERVIEW OF VALLEYS

There are 5 things you and I need to remember about valleys in our spiritual life.

1. VALLEYS ARE INEVITABLE.

Jesus said that "in this world, you shall have tribulation" (John 16:33). Mark it down. God has already planned valleys on your calendar because that is where we grow the most, not on the mountain top.

2. VALLEYS ARE UNPREDICTABLE.

Jeremiah said that "disaster follows disaster; the whole land lies in ruins. In an instant my tents are destroyed" (Jeremiah 4:20). Our lives can be thrust into a valley in a moment.

3. VALLEYS ARE IMPARTIAL.

Jesus told us in Matthew 5:45 that "it rains on the just and the unjust" and not just the just! Unbelievers have plenty of troubles, too.

4. VALLEYS ARE TEMPORARY.

Solomon reminds us that there is a season to all things. There is a season to rejoice and a season of suffering. But, the good thing is that they are both short-lived. The clouds come, the storm hits and the SON appears (I Peter 1:6).

5. VALLEYS GROW OUR FAITH.

James 1:1-4 declares that believers in Christ should actually rejoice and praise God when trials come because God is answering our prayer and growing our faith! Did you ask the Lord to help you to become more like Jesus? Did you ask the Father to strengthen your faith?

If you are in a valley... it is not a disappointment, it is HIS APPOINTMENT.

DON'T WASTE YOUR VALLEYS!

I believe many of us have spent our time on this earth missing a blessing in disguise. We have wasted our valleys! We have complained to the Lord when He put us in a valley, not understanding that it was sent to bless us and to lead us to the mountain top.

How can we waste our valleys?

1. We can waste our valley if we do not believe it was designed for us by God Himself.

2. We can waste our valley if we think it is a curse from Satan and not a gift from Heaven.

3. We can waste our valley if we spend too much time WORRYING about the valley and not enough time WORSHIPPING Jesus.

4. We can waste our valley if we allow it to drive us into solitude and self-pity instead of allowing it to deepen our relationships with those whom God has planted around us.

5. We can waste our valley if we grieve as unbelievers who have no hope.

6. We can waste our valley if we treat sin as casually as we did before we experienced this valley.

7. We can waste our valley if we fail to use this painful trial as a means of witnessing to unbelievers of the glory of God and the power of faith in Christ to overcome.

ARE YOU WASTING A VALLEY RIGHT NOW?

NO RAIN ---- NO GAIN.

Chile is a beautiful country with beautiful people. However, the northern part of Chile contains one of the driest places on the globe known as the Atacama Desert.

It never rains there. They have plenty of sunshine, plenty of warmth.......and very few things grow there because there is no rain.

If you are going to grow in Christ, you must walk through valleys. But, the awesome truth is that you never walk alone in your valley for "You are with me".

"THE VALLEY OF THE SHADOW OF DEATH" (Hinnom Valley)

The Hinnom Valley was where horrific things took place. Pagans worshipped the god named Molech there, and, as part of their worship, they would take their babies and children to sacrifice them to a god who was really a demonic spirit. This is the practice the Bible calls "passing through the fire" (Deut 18:10). The children were burned alive or sacrificed and then their bodies burned and placed into the Valley of Hinnom.

After the Jews returned to Israel from the Babylonian exile, Hinnom became a garbage dump where anything considered unclean was put. Dead animals & bodies of executed criminals would be put there, along with all trash. Fires had to be burned here non-stop so the waste would not take over.

Because of the smoke and the darkness, this valley was dark, difficult and scary to pass through. *It was often so dark, it is said one could not see his hand in front of his face.*

When Jesus taught about eternity in Hell, He used the word, Gehenna, meaning "a place of waste."

Wasted lives.
Wasted grace.
Wasted opportunity.
Wasted time.

It is also interesting to think that when Jesus taught about faith He compared it to the Mustard seed. Ironically, Mustard trees grew everywhere in the Valley of Hinnom. We know that Jesus meant that, even though faith is small, it can accomplish big things. But, think about this. To think that a miniscule mustard seed could grow itself through the darkness, death and waste of the Valley of Hinnom is a picture of triumphant faith!

"I FEAR NO EVIL......FOR YOU ARE WITH ME"

I have witnessed the death of so many who walked with their Shepherd to their Heavenly Home. The peace on their faces as they crossed over into Glory has been an incredible miracle for me to behold throughout my ministry.

The opposite is true for those who do not know Christ and come to their last breath fearing evil. Here are some amazing quotes of unbelievers who walked through the valley of the shadow of death and were filled with fear:

Caesar Borgia: *"While I lived, I provided for everything but death; now I must die, and I am unprepared to die."*

Thomas Hobbs, political philosopher *"I say again, if I had the whole world at my disposal, I would give it to live one day. I am about to take a leap into the dark."*

Thomas Payne, the leading atheistic writer in *American colonies: "Stay with me, for God's sake; I cannot bear to be left alone; O Lord, help me! I would give worlds, if I had them, that The Age of Reason had never been published."*

Sir Thomas Scott, Chancellor of England: *"Until this moment, I thought there was neither a God nor a hell. Now I know and feel that there are both, and I am doomed to perdition."*

Robert Ingersoll: *"O God, if there be a God, save my soul, if I have a soul!"*

But, oh, the difference when a child of God who knows where he is going comes to the chilly banks of the Jordan and is preparing to pass through to be with their Shepherd. Listen to the deathbed confession of the great preacher from Chicago, D.L. Moody:

"Earth recedes. Heaven opens before me. If this is death, it is sweet! There is no valley here. God is calling me, and I must go."

*Are you ready to make your eternal journey?
Do you know where you are going for eternity?
Do you know the Shepherd?*

*I heard an old story about a king one time who had a court Jester who entertained him marvelously. One day he said to the court jester, "O, court jester, you are the biggest fool I know." He extended to him his royal scepter. He said, **"Keep it until you find a bigger fool than yourself."***

For years, the court jester kept the royal scepter of the king. Then the days came when the king knew he was going to die. He found himself upon his deathbed never again to arise. He called for his court jester to come in and he said, "O court jester, I am going on a long journey, never again to return."

The court jester said, "O, sir, what preparations have you made for this long journey?" The king shook his head and said, "Alas, I've made none."

In that moment the jester extended to the king his scepter. He said, "Here sir, you are a bigger fool than I."

Make sure you have your reservations for eternity. Trust Christ as your Savior today by inviting Him into your life.

John 1:12 – "To as many as received Jesus, to them God gave the right to be called the children of God by believing on His Name."

*Thank you for spending
a little time with me walking
through the valley together.
Keep your eyes on the Shepherd.*

Larry Petton

Watch My Interview with A Shepherd

Garris Hudson is our awesome Student Pastor & Media Director at Cross Pointe Community Church in Tontitown, AR. He created a great video of my interview with a shepherd and has made it available for your viewing. Just go to YouTube and type: "To Be A Shepherd – Cross Pointe" and you can see it.